Career Struggles?

Don Barnes

Published by Don Barnes, 2024.

 **LifeWorksInThrees.com**

Table of Contents

About the Author

Don is the founder and author of Life Works in Threes!™ E-books. He is a lifelong Texan who has traveled extensively while taking a keen interest in human behavior. His curiosity about life and what drives humans led him to the discovery of how life works in threes. He coined this term as the *Tryune Concept*.

Don attended college on an athletic scholarship and then embarked on a 30-year career in the oil and gas industry. Since the year 2000, he has been a consultant for distributors and manufacturers of various industries. Along the way, he worked on his Tryune discovery in hopes of someday sharing his findings with those struggling unnecessarily... in life. What Don surmised from 40+ years of R&D was that people were struggling unnecessarily because they were not aware that "life works in threes." They, for the most part, have been living their lives <u>by chance</u> rather than <u>by choice,</u> he also discovered.

From this, he began focusing on the "mechanics of life" which shows formulas for success with subjects such as *life, health, money, purpose and so forth.* When people are able to grasp the Tryune Concept, they can apply the formulas with topics that interest them and begin eliminating the struggle. This epiphany is what triggered his Tryune venture and is now on the path of sharing with all who desire to improve on their lives.

Don currently resides in Southern California and Texas while overseeing his businesses and investments.

Life Works in Threes™

When I was a kid growing up, no one sat me down and said, "Okay Don, I'm going to show you how life works so that you can navigate your way through adulthood." I graduated from school, got married and went about my way with the "learn as you go" concept. It was kind of like putting together a backyard swing set without a set of instructions. Lots of frustration and do-overs, for sure!

My discovery of the "triune" word and noticing how things come together in threes is really what set me off on researching that maybe "life comes in three" ...sort of a mechanical approach to managing life, if you will. I combed the libraries and bookstores for information on this and found one book on the subject that was written back in 1951. The author's name was John S. Arant.

What Mr. Arant had to say is this "For lack of a better name, I have called this *The Triangle of Triumph* and therefore, consistent with the name, since most of these conclusions are built on the geometric figure of the triangle." He continued "All Life and all lives are seated in, and circumscribed by, the triangle. The Author and Source and Director of all life is Himself triune in character – Father, Son, and Holy Spirit. Man is of triple nature – body, mind, and spirit – and within those three there are many triangles – desires, development, decay; intellect, will, sensibilities. Of this "paced interlude in the midst of eternity" which we call time there is the triangle of Past, Present, and Future. Space – that limitless and measureless element of the physical universe – is best known in terms of Height, Breadth, and Depth. Try building yourself some triangles along the lines of your Will, your Work, your Way – You will find some interesting angles.

So, for the first time, I realized that life is designed in a mechanical way to come in threes. That means you don't have to rely on wishing and hoping things turn out okay. You can actually look at the three parts that a particular thing is made of and then apply them to get what you're wanting. Like a three-ingredient recipe or a combination lock. With a combination lock, you need the three exact numbers to unlock the lock...otherwise you will continue to struggle.

Some 40 years later, I accumulated things that work in threes and that's when I knew I needed to share this with anyone wanting answers. To have success/harmony in your life, just apply the three parts of an area you're working on, and things will fall into place. I also learned that the recipe for success with just about anything is by doing these three things, consistently – THINK positively, SPEAK positively and ACT positively. For example, if I want to be a successful artist. I would think to myself "I can do this because I have the talent." Then I would speak it this way "Yes, I am working on my art degree and plan to do portraits professionally." Finally, I would act on that by taking art classes and continue crafting my skill. Eventually, I will see the positive results/ success I'm looking for.

Conversely, if I think positively but speak negatively...it will cancel out. Or if I speak positively but have no positive action going on...nothing will happen.

I looked up "How Life Works" and "The Mechanics of Life" and these are really talking about the biology of how our cells work and other chemistry. TRYUNE WORKS! teaches that life is kind of like building blocks. Pick a topic you may be struggling with. See the three parts that topic consists of and then start applying them...on a consistent basis. That will help you overcome the struggle and get you back in harmony/ success with how life works.

For 30+ years I was a golf instructor (by accident). My two kids had some success playing junior golf and so friends and neighbors would ask me to show them and their kids how to play golf successfully. From all of this, I got pretty good at watching golfers on the driving range and could spot right away why they were struggling with hitting bad golf shots. I was able to do that because I knew the three steps to hitting good golf shots. I learned them from studying golf and played for several decades. I "broke the code" for me so to speak.

So now you know that life works in threes. You can live your life *by choice* rather than *by chance* and that my friend... is the key to a fulfilling life.

My sanctuary on the Pacific coast

Introduction

Choosing the right career path can be a game-changer in your life! When you find a career that aligns with your skills, interests, and values, it's like discovering a perfect fit for your professional journey. One of the biggest benefits is that you'll likely find more fulfillment and satisfaction in your work. Imagine waking up excited about what the day holds because you genuinely enjoy what you do. Whether it's helping others, solving complex problems, or creating something new, a career that resonates with you can bring a sense of purpose and joy that spills over into other aspects of your life.

Another great perk is the potential for growth and advancement. When you're in a career that suits you well, you're more likely to excel and progress. You'll probably find yourself eager to learn, take on new challenges, and develop your skills further. This not only boosts your confidence but also opens opportunities for promotions, raises, and professional recognition. Plus, when you're passionate about your work, you tend to go the extra mile, which employers and clients notice and appreciate.

Let's not forget the impact on your overall well-being. Studies show that being in the right career can positively influence your mental and emotional health. Lower stress levels, improved self-esteem, and a better work-life balance are just some of the benefits you might experience. When work feels less like a chore and more like a calling, it can enhance your overall quality of life. So, take the time to explore your options, consider your strengths and interests, and aim for a career that brings out the best in you. Your future self will thank you for it!

My discovery of the Tryune Concept

Before we dive into career struggles and how to overcome them, let me share my discovery of the Tryune Concept and how life works in threes. It all began in the summer of 1982.

I grew up with parents who treated everyone with decency and respect. My three older sisters and I were raised in a home that was "middle-class traditional." We lived in modest homes in different small towns, attended school and church on a regular basis and celebrated all the traditional holidays. Eventually we settled during the spring of 1964 in the big city of Houston, Texas. I'll never forget the vastness of the city and hearing sirens from police cars, fire trucks and ambulances on a regular basis. I was excited and scared at the same time.

Once settled in this fast-paced city, I finished my growing-up years with an academic diploma and sweetheart intact. I got a job, bought a car, got married, bought a house and produced two beautiful babies in a span of about 5 years. Talk about having to grow up fast!

Things went from great in my childhood to absolute misery in my young adulthood. I began to struggle with my job because deep down I just hated what I was doing. This problem created a snowball effect because soon after, my weight, my finances, my relationships, my happiness and everything else worth saving was going down the drain. I eventually hit a level of frustration that I had never experienced before and didn't know how to get out of it. My cry for help was for anyone or anything to come to my rescue. I just ran out of solutions for my situation.

This is when my discovery happened.

One night shortly after my meltdown, while sleeping soundly, the word "triune" began to softly pound in my head like a mantra. I woke up a little startled and decided to go look up the word in my favorite dictionary (this was WAY before Google.) The definition said '**triune** (try-une) – 1) a group of three things; united. 2) Being 3 in 1 such as *humans are mental, physical and spiritual.* I scratched my head, got a glass of water and went back to bed.

The next day while driving around town, I began thinking about things that I was taught in my younger years that came in threes. My Boy Scout manual taught that to have **character**, I needed to be *1) physically strong, 2) mentally awake and 3) morally straight.* My high school football coach would say emphatically "If you want to be **a good football player**, you have to be *1) mobile 2) agile and 3) hostile!*" My first sales manager shared with me that to be **a successful salesman**, I needed to have *1) sales skills, 2) product knowledge and 3) a good image.*

"Hmm", I thought, "wonder if there are other examples out there of things that work in threes?" So, some 40 years later, I have researched and discovered that many, many things work in threes. What this message was telling me is that to achieve success or balance in any significant area of my life, the three things that area consisted of had to be present, continuously. That's when I had my epiphany. This discovery was telling me the secret to how life <u>really</u> works...in a mechanical way.

Tryune is a play on the word "triune" as an invitation to "try" this concept. Furthermore, we do not say that life <u>only</u> works in threes. Life also works in ones, twos, fours and so on. What has been observed though is that the many things significant to life, just so happen to come and work in threes. That's what is being shared in this book.

Now, you are about to see 40+ years of research and proof that life works in threes. I did not make up any of these topics. I invite you to research them on the internet to validate what is written here. There are some interesting facts that most of us have never realized...until now.

How Life Works in Threes (around 200 examples)

<u>LIFE</u>

Humans consist of *body, mind and soul.*

A human's basic needs are *health, income and provisions.*

A human's basic wants are *comfort, gain and approval.*

Our minds are made up of the *conscious, the subconscious and the unconscious.*

Philosophy explains *the id, the ego and superego.*

Atoms consist of *protons, neutrons and electrons.*

Motion is explained by *three basic laws.*

Science falls under three main branches: *natural, social and formal sciences*

Time is *past, present and future...*at the same time.

Electricity consists of *ohms, amperes and voltage.*

Music's basic elements are *duration, pitch and timbre.*

Democracy is a government *of the people, by the people and for the people.*

U.S. branches of government are *the judicial, the executive and the legislative.*

Armed Forces protect us on *land, air and sea.*

Environmentally, we are asked *to reduce, recycle and re-use.*

The news program gives us *the news, sports and conditions.*

Our days consist of *morning, afternoon and evening.*

Three months in each season of the year

Our main meals are known as *breakfast, lunch and dinner.*

A balanced diet consists of *good proteins, carbohydrates and fats.*

Traditional Family consists of *father, mother, and child(ren)*

<u>SCIENCES</u>

Three major branches of natural science – *(physical, earth/ space and life sciences)*

Three major branches of modern physics - *(classical, relativistic, quantum)*

Three major branches of biology *(botany, zoology, microbiology)*

Three spatial dimensions: *height* (up/down), *width* (left/ right) and *depth* (forwards/backwards)

Three-gauge bosons (photon, gluon, W&Z bosons)

Three types of elementary particles *(leptons, quarks, gauge bosons)*

Three quarks in every proton *(two "up" and one "down")*

Three primary colors of light *(red, green, blue)*

Three color tone properties *(hue, value, chroma)*

Three laws of motion (*Newton's laws*)

Three laws of planetary motion (*Kepler's laws*)

Three layers of the Sun's interior (*core, radiative zone, convective zone*)

Three layers of the Sun's atmosphere (*photosphere, chromosphere, corona*)

Three types of meteorites (*iron, stony iron, stony*)

Three types of galaxy shapes (*elliptical, spiral, irregular*)

Three substances of the universe (*normal matter, 'dark matter', 'dark energy'*)

Three phases of the moon (*new moon, first quarter, full moon*)

Three planetary regions (*temperate, sub-tropical, tropical*)

Three layers of the Earth (*crust, mantle, core*)

Three components of an ecosystem (*producers, consumers, decomposers*)

Three types of rocks (*igneous, sedimentary, metamorphic*)

Three types of fossil fuels (*coal, crude oil, natural gas*)

Three hydrological processes (*evaporation, condensation, precipitation*)

Three basic types of (meteorological) precipitation (*liquid, freezing, frozen*)

Three types of substances *(mono-constituent, multi-constituent, UVCB)*

Three phases of (normal) matter *(solid, liquid, gas)*

Three types of covalent chemical bonds *(single, double and triple bonds)*

Three isotopes of hydrogen *(protium, deuterium, tritium)*

Three atoms in each molecule of water *(two hydrogen atoms and an oxygen atom)*

Three endings to salts *(-ide, -ite, -ate)*

Three requirements for fire *(fuel, oxygen, heat)*

Three nucleotide bases in a genetic codon

Three domains of life *(archaea, bacteria and eukaryotes)*

Three major groups of flowering plants *(monocots, eudicots, magnolids)*

Three major functions that are basic to plant growth and development: *(photosynthesis* [making sugars], *respiration* [metabolizing those sugars], and *transpiration* [water vapor loss]

Three things that the chlorophyll in plants needs for photosynthesis to take place: *(sunlight, carbon dioxide and water)*

Transpiration serves three roles: *(cooling the plant, moving minerals* and *sugars through the plant,* and *maintaining the turgidity pressure* [stiffness] *of the plant's cells)*

Three parts of an insect's body *(head, thorax, abdomen)*

BIOLOGY

Three types of cones in the retina, relating to the three primary colors

Three semi-circular canals in the ear *(lateral, anterior, posterior)*

Three sections in the ear *(outer, middle, inner)*

Three ossicles in the middle ear *(malleus, incus, stapes)*

Three segments to each limb *(proximal, mid, distal)*

Three bones in each arm *(humerus, radius, ulna)*

Three joints in the arm *(shoulder, elbow, wrist)*

Three joints in the leg *(hip, knee, ankle)*

Three joints in the elbow *(humeroulnar, humeroradial, proximal radioulnar)*

Three functional compartments in the knee joint *(the femoropatellar, medial femorotibial* and *lateral femorotibial articulations)*

Three types of fibrous joints *(sutures, gomphoses, syndesmoses)*

Three types of bone in each hand (*carpals, metacarpals, phalanges*)

Three types of bone in each foot (*tarsals, metatarsals, phalanges*)

Three bones (phalanges) in each finger and in each toe (*proximal, intermediate, distal*)

Three layers of skin (*dermis, epidermis, hypodermis*)

Three components of a cell (*cell membrane, nucleus, cytoplasm*)

Three types of blood vessels (*arteries, veins, capillaries*)

Three types of blood cells [*red* (erythrocytes), *white* (leukocytes), *platelets* (thrombocytes)]

Three processes of the intestinal tract (*ingestion, digestion, excretion*)

Three germ layers (*Endoderm, Mesoderm, Ectoderm*)

Three parts of a human tooth (*crown, neck, root*)

Three organs of otolaryngology (*ear, nose, throat*)

Three major body systems (*digestive, circulatory, respiratory*)

Three parts to a neuron: (*soma* [*cell body*], *axon, dendrites*)

Three main parts of the brain (*forebrain, midbrain, hindbrain*)

Three parts of the forebrain *(cerebrum, thalamus, hypothalamus)*

Three parts of the midbrain *(colliculi, tegmentum, cerebral peduncles)*

Three parts of the hindbrain *(cerebellum, pons, medulla)*

Three membranes enclosing the brain *(dura mater, arachnoid, pia mater)*

The brain operates on three levels: *consciously* (for cognitive thought and declarative memory); *subconsciously* (for pre-planned actions and procedural memory); and *unconsciously* (for breathing, heart beating, etc.)

Our conscious mind is fed from three sources: *our senses* (which can be fooled); *our memory* (which is flawed); and *our imagination* (which is inventive)

Three aspects of the human mind *(memory, intellect, will)*

Three parts of the human personality *(id, ego, superego)*

The sum of human capacity consists of three abilities *(thought, word and deed)*

Three times of man *(birth, life, death)*

Three periods of the Gait Cycle *(initial double limb support, single limb support, and terminal double limb support)*

<u>MUSIC</u>

Three types of musical notes *(sharps, flats, naturals)*

Three aspects of a song (*lyrics, melody, rhythm*)

Three types of musical chords (*root, third, fifth*)

<u>MATHEMATICS</u>

Three types of a real number (*positive, negative, zero*)

Three parts to any arithmetic operation: for addition: *augend, addend and sum* - for subtraction: *minuend, subtrahend and difference* - for multiplication: *multiplicand, multiplier and product* - for division: *dividend, divisor and quotient*

Three laws of arithmetic operations (*commutative, associative, distributive*)

Three types of equivalence relation (*reflexivity, symmetry, transitivity*)

Three types of symmetry operations (*translation, rotation, reflection*)

Three geometries (*Euclidean, spherical, hyperbolic*)

The number 3 is the basis of an entire branch of mathematics, called trigonometry (from the Greek *trigonon* "triangle" + *metron* "measure")

Three trigonometric functions (*sine, cosine, tangent*)

Three types of average (*mean, mode, median*)

<u>GRAMMAR</u>

Three logical operators (*AND, OR and NOT*)

Three laws of logic (*identity, noncontradiction, excluded middle*)

Three parts of a logical syllogism (*major premise, minor premise, conclusion*)

Three grammatical parts to a sentence (*subject, verb, complement*)

Three persons in grammar [*1st person* (I/we), *2nd* (you or your), *3rd* (he/she/it/they)]

Three genders in grammar [*masculine* (he/him), *feminine* (she/her), *neuter* (it)]

Three forms of comparison in grammar [*positive, comparative* (more, -er), *superlative* (most, -est)]

Three cases in (English) grammar [*subjective/nominative* (he), *objective/accusative* (him) and *possessive/genitive* (his)]

Three parts of a narrative (*beginning, middle, end*)

Components of an essay (*introduction, body, conclusion*)

Elements of a rhetorical appeal (*ethos, pathos, logos*)

Aspects of a story (*plot, characters, setting*)

<u>RELIGION</u>

The Creator – *omniscient, omnipotent, omnipresent*

Christian God – *Father, Son, Holy Spirit*

Jesus – *The Way, The Truth, The Life*

Ancient Near East- *Qudshu, Astarte, Anat*

Classical Antiquity – Many dieties came in threes

Hinduism – Para Brahman is *Brahma, Visnu, Shiva*

Ancient Celtic Cultures – *many example of triad dieties*

Buddhism – *The three jewels*

Taoism – *The three pure ones*

Islam – *Fear, Hope and Love*

Baha'i - *Intention, Power and Action*

Confucianism – *Benevolence, Wisdom and Courage*

<u>OTHER TRIUNE EXAMPLES</u>

3 Coins in a Fountain

3 Days of the Condor

3 Miles in a League

3 Goals in a Hat Trick

3 Piece Suit

3 Feet in a Yard

3 Books in Lord of the Rings

3 Ring Circus

3 Ships of Christopher Columbus

3 Sheets to the Wind

3 Books in a Trilogy

3 Wheels on a Tricycle

3 Wise Men

3-Legged Race

3 Ring Circus

3-Wheeler

3 Cornered Hat

3 Dimensional

3 Musketeers

3 R's (reading, 'riting, 'rithmatic)

3 Sides of a triangle

3 Races in the Triple Crown (horse racing)

3 Angles in a Triangle

3 Trimesters in a Pregnancy

3 Flavors in Neapolitan Ice Cream

3 Stars in Orion's belt

3 Barleycorns in an Inch

3 Hands on a Clock (with the Seconds Hand)

3 Colors in a Flag

3 Minute Egg

3 Great Pyramids at Giza

3 Holes in a Bowling Ball

3 Colors in a Set of Traffic Lights

3 Minutes in a Boxing Round

3 Teaspoons in a Tablespoon

3 Legs on a Stool

3 Monastic Vows (Obience, Stability, Conversatio Morum)

3 Body Types: Endomorph, Mesomorph, Ectomorph

3 Ring Notebooks

3 Germ layers: Endoderm, Mesoderm, Ectoderm

3 Species of Homo: Homo habilis, Homo erectus, Homo sapiens

3 Basic parts of a camera: Lens, Shutter, Sensor

3 Stages of a Project lifecycle: initiation, planning, execution

The Truth, The Whole Truth and Nothing but the Truth

Life, Liberty and the Pursuit of Happiness

Hear no Evil, See no Evil, Speak no Evil

National motto of France/Haiti: Liberty, Equality, Fraternity

Paper, Rock, Scissors

Ready, Aim, Fire

On Your mark, Get Set, Go

Olympic medals of gold, silver, bronze

Types of joints (ball & socket, hinge, pivot)

Stages of a rocket launch (launch, orbit, re-entry)

Parts of a joke (setup, delivery, punchline)

Primary components of a transistor (emitter, base, collector)

Primary components of an airplane (fuselage, wings, empennage)

Basic components of a computer: CPU, memory, storage

Three phases in the development of technology (*eotechnic* [*mechanical*], *paleotechnic* [*steam-powered*] and *neotechnic* [*electric-powered*]

Communication systems require three components (*transmitter, channel, receiver*)

The list goes on. See if you can find more examples as they are everywhere in our universe. Now that you know that life works in threes (with proof!), we can begin to apply this concept to whatever topics we want.

So, to overcome struggles in career, we need to apply the three areas that career consist of – YOU, INDUSTRIES and YOUR MISSION. Let's get started!

YOU
CAREER
INDUSTRIES
YOUR
MISSION

CAREER

Have you ever thought about how much time we spend working over a lifetime? It's quite a chunk! On average, most people spend about a third of their lives at work. That's around 90,000 hours (about 10 and a half years) during a typical career span. It might sound like a lot, but it's also a big part of what shapes our daily routines, our relationships, and even our sense of identity. When you consider how much time we invest in our careers, it becomes clear why finding a job that brings you fulfillment and satisfaction is so important.

But here's the cool part: those hours don't have to feel like a drag! When you're in a career that aligns with your passions and interests, it can make that time more enjoyable and meaningful. Whether you're helping others, innovating new ideas, or mastering a skill you love, each day can feel like an opportunity to grow and contribute. So, while work takes up a significant portion of our lives, it also has the potential to be a source of fulfillment and personal growth.

Plus, the time spent at work isn't just about earning a paycheck (though that's important!). It's also about the connections we make, the skills we develop, and the impact we have on our communities. When you're engaged in work that you find meaningful, those hours can fly by as you tackle challenges, collaborate with inspiring colleagues, and see your efforts make a difference. So, whether you're just starting out or contemplating a career change, remember that the time you invest in your career isn't just about the clock—it's about creating a life that you're excited to live every day.

It is amusing to me that there are career counselors in high school...like an 18-year-old knows what he/she wants to do with the rest of their lives! I was 50 years old before I knew exactly what I wanted to do career-wise. It helped that I spent the previous 30 years working in various occupations before finally getting a grip on what interested me the most.

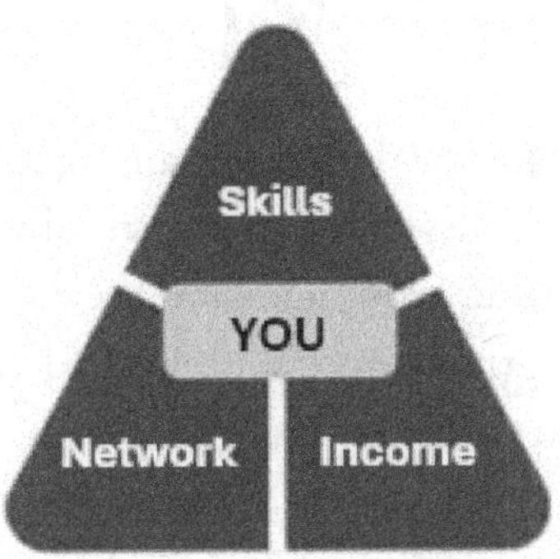
Skills
YOU
Network
Income

YOU

Entering or re-entering the workforce is an exciting adventure, and part of that journey involves assessing your own abilities. It's like taking a snapshot of what makes you awesome! One of the first steps is recognizing your strengths—those skills and talents that come naturally to you and set you apart. Maybe you're a fantastic problem solver, a great communicator, or someone who thrives under pressure. Identifying these strengths can help you pinpoint roles and industries where you can shine.

But it's not just about strengths; it's also about areas for growth. Assessing your abilities means being honest about where you might need to develop or learn more. Maybe you're eager to improve your technical skills, expand your knowledge in a specific field, or enhance your leadership abilities. Acknowledging these areas gives you a roadmap for personal and professional growth, setting you up for success as you navigate the job market.

Another crucial aspect of self-assessment is understanding your passions and interests. What gets you excited? What activities make you lose track of time? Your interests can guide you towards careers that align with your values and bring you fulfillment. Whether it's working with people, crunching numbers, creating art, or analyzing data, knowing what sparks your enthusiasm can steer you towards a career path that feels rewarding and meaningful. So, take the time to reflect on your abilities, both strengths and areas for growth, and consider how they can shape your journey into the workforce. Your unique blend of skills and passions has the power to open doors to a career that's not just a job, but a source of joy and fulfillment.

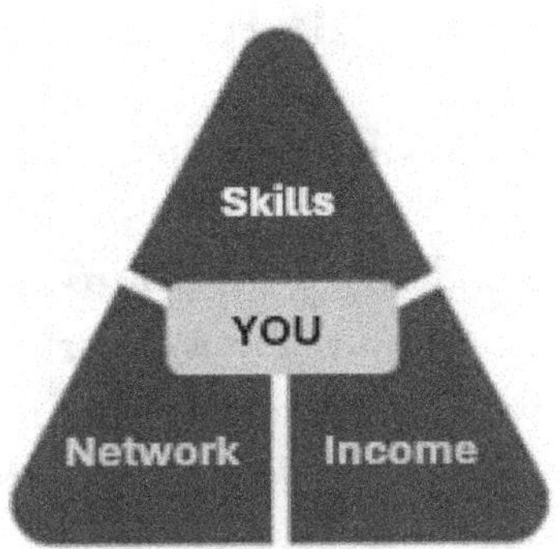
Skills
YOU
Network
Income

Skills

Here's a list of preferred job skills that employers often look for:

1. **Communication Skills**: Being able to articulate ideas clearly, whether in writing or verbally, is crucial. It helps in collaborating with colleagues, presenting ideas to clients, and handling customer inquiries effectively.
2. **Adaptability**: The ability to quickly adjust to new situations, technologies, or environments shows employers that you can thrive in a dynamic workplace.
3. **Problem-Solving**: Employers value individuals who can analyze issues, identify solutions, and implement effective strategies to overcome challenges.
4. **Teamwork**: Collaboration is key in most workplaces. Employers appreciate team players who can work well with others, contribute ideas, and support group efforts.
5. **Leadership**: Even if you're not in a managerial role, demonstrating leadership qualities like initiative, decision-making, and motivating others can set you apart.
6. **Time Management**: Being able to prioritize tasks, meet deadlines, and efficiently manage your workload shows employers that you can handle responsibilities effectively.
7. **Technical Skills**: Depending on the industry, proficiency in specific software, programming languages, or technical tools relevant to the job is often highly valued.
8. **Attention to Detail**: Whether it's proofreading documents, analyzing data, or managing finances, employers appreciate candidates who can maintain accuracy and thoroughness in their work.
9. **Customer Service**: For roles involving client interaction, having strong customer service skills—such as empathy,

patience, and problem-solving—can make a big difference.

10. **Creativity**: Bringing fresh ideas, innovative solutions, and a creative approach to tasks or projects demonstrates your ability to think outside the box and drive innovation.

Remember, every job and industry may emphasize different skills, so tailoring your skill set to match the specific requirements of the role you're applying for can greatly enhance your chances of success.

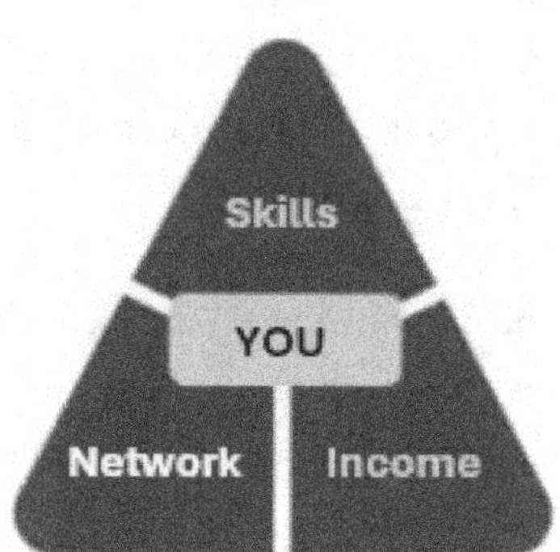
Skills
YOU
Network
Income

Network

When I was in high school, I would hear so often that "You need a college degree to get a good job." What I found out from experience is that the college degree is not as important as the network that is built in college with fraternities and sororities. This is the beginning of a powerful network. If you want to get a head start or increase your chances of job selection, make your networking a priority.

The old saying "It's not what you know but who you know." has a lot of merit. In the oil and gas industry that I was a part of because of my grandfather, my uncles and my father...made my life a whole lot easier than others in my age group. A stranger coming into that industry, without a friend, will have a long road ahead of them, for sure.

Having a solid network of industry contacts can be like having a secret weapon in your career arsenal—it opens doors and creates opportunities you might not find otherwise. Imagine being able to tap into a pool of professionals who can offer advice, provide job leads, or even recommend you for positions within their companies. These connections can give you insider knowledge about job openings, industry trends, and upcoming projects, giving you a competitive edge in your job search or career advancement.

Building and maintaining relationships within your industry isn't just about immediate gains; it's about long-term benefits too. As you nurture these connections over time, you cultivate a reputation as someone who is reliable, knowledgeable, and connected. This can lead to referrals, collaborations on exciting projects, and invitations to industry events where you can continue to expand your network. Ultimately, having a strong network of industry contacts isn't just about who you know—it's about the support, advice, and opportunities they can provide throughout your professional journey. So, whether you're just starting out or looking to climb the career ladder, investing in relationships within your industry can pay off in ways that extend far beyond your initial expectations.

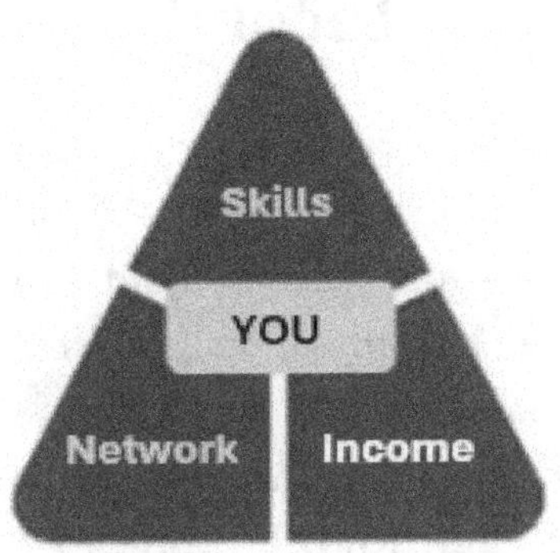

Skills
YOU
Network
Income

Income

Over the years there have been books written with titles such as "Do what you love, and the money will follow." That is nonsense to believe that. If I love to fish, play golf, crochet, build things out of wood and so on. The chances are slim to none of making a real living doing that. So, let's get real about income...which is why we work in the first place.

Living on a **guaranteed income** can offer a sense of security and stability, which is a huge pro. Knowing you have a steady flow of income can alleviate financial stress and provide peace of mind, allowing you to focus on other aspects of life such as pursuing hobbies, spending time with loved ones, or furthering your education. It can also provide a foundation for planning ahead and making long-term financial decisions with confidence. However, one potential drawback is the risk of complacency or lack of motivation to seek additional sources of income or pursue career advancement. While guaranteed income ensures basic needs are met, it may not always align with ambitious career goals or aspirations for higher earnings.

Having a **guaranteed income while pursuing a side hustle** can offer the best of both worlds! It provides the stability of a steady paycheck while allowing you to explore your passions, enhance your skills, and potentially increase your earnings on the side. A side hustle can be a creative outlet where you can turn hobbies or interests into additional income streams. It also offers flexibility—you can choose how much time and effort to dedicate to your side hustle, making it manageable alongside your primary job. This combination allows you to diversify your income sources, build valuable experience, and maintain financial security, all while pursuing your entrepreneurial spirit. Balancing a guaranteed income with a side hustle can create a rewarding and fulfilling path where you can thrive both professionally and personally.

Entering a **full commission job** comes with its own set of risks and rewards, much like diving into an exciting adventure! On the reward side, the potential for earnings is often uncapped—you can directly influence your income based on your performance and sales achievements. This can be incredibly motivating and rewarding, especially if you excel at building relationships, closing deals, and meeting targets. Moreover, success in a commission-based role often brings recognition and the satisfaction of knowing your hard work directly translates into financial rewards. However, the risk lies in the variability of income. Your earnings can fluctuate month to month depending on market conditions, client preferences, and other factors beyond your control. It requires resilience, strategic planning, and sometimes a longer ramp-up period to establish a consistent income stream. This is a legitimate way to gamble. If you're good, you'll make great money. If not, it can be a long, hard road.

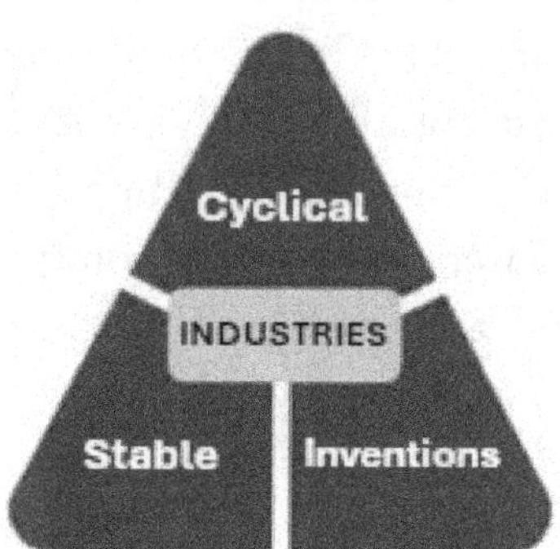
Cyclical
INDUSTRIES
Stable
Inventions

INDUSTRIES

Choosing to work in a stable industry can be a wise career move that offers security and peace of mind. Industries like healthcare, education, and certain sectors of technology often demonstrate resilience even during economic downturns. Stability in an industry means there's typically steady demand for goods or services, which translates to more consistent job opportunities and less vulnerability to market fluctuations. This can provide a sense of stability in your career trajectory, reducing the uncertainty that comes with more volatile industries.

Moreover, stable industries often offer opportunities for long-term growth and advancement. Companies within these sectors tend to invest in employee development, provide competitive benefits, and foster a supportive work environment. This commitment to stability can lead to greater job satisfaction and loyalty among employees, as well as opportunities to hone specialized skills and expertise that are highly valued within the industry.

However, it's essential to research and assess the specific subsectors within an industry to understand its stability and growth potential. Some industries may face challenges due to technological advancements, regulatory changes, or shifts in consumer behavior. Keeping abreast of industry trends and continuously updating your skills can help you navigate potential changes and position yourself effectively within a stable industry. Ultimately, picking a stable industry aligns with the goal of building a resilient and fulfilling career path where you can thrive and grow over the long term.

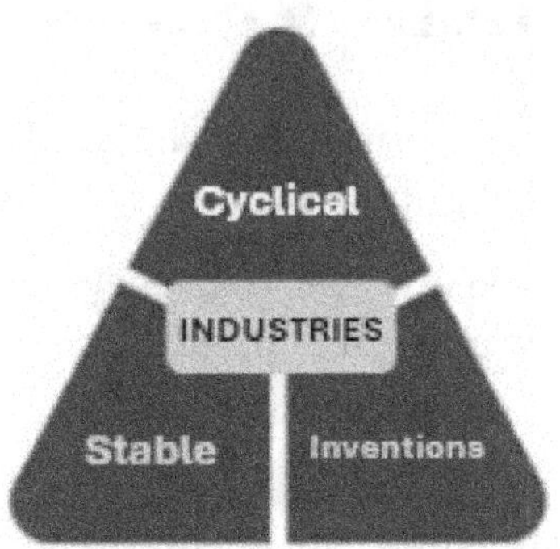
Cyclical
INDUSTRIES
Stable
Inventions

Cyclical

Cyclical industries are those whose performance and demand tend to fluctuate in response to economic conditions. Some examples of cyclical industries include:

1. **Automotive Industry**: Sales of cars and vehicles often rise and fall with economic cycles.
2. **Construction Industry**: Construction activities, including residential and commercial building projects, tend to follow economic cycles closely.
3. **Travel and Tourism**: The travel and tourism industry is highly sensitive to economic conditions and consumer confidence.
4. **Retail Industry**: Retail sales can be cyclical, particularly for non-essential goods and luxury items.
5. **Manufacturing Industry**: Certain segments of the manufacturing sector, such as durable goods like appliances and electronics, can be cyclical.
6. Oil and Gas Industry: Fluctuating prices for crude oil cause this industry to go up and down...resulting in job layoffs on a regular basis.

Understanding the cyclical nature of these industries can help businesses and individuals better prepare for economic fluctuations and adapt their strategies accordingly. Supplementing cyclical jobs with side hustles can be a savvy strategy to smooth out income fluctuations and expand your skills and opportunities. In cyclical industries like construction or retail, where workloads and earnings can vary seasonally or with economic cycles, having a side hustle offers a reliable way to generate additional income during slower periods. Whether it's freelancing in a creative field, offering consulting services related to your expertise, or starting a small business, a side hustle can provide financial stability and flexibility.

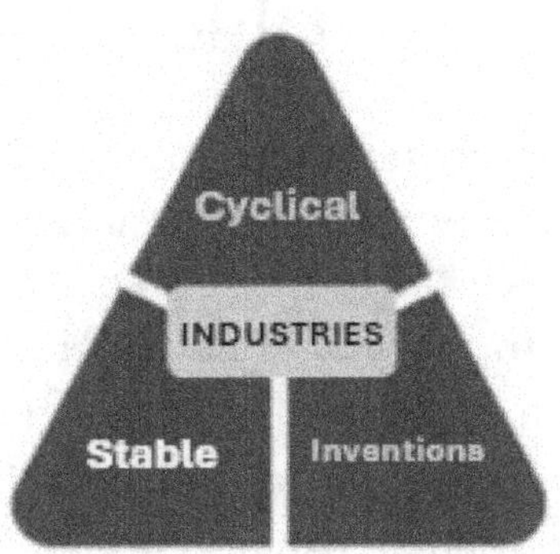
Cyclical
INDUSTRIES
Stable
Inventions

Stable

Here's a list of some stable industries that typically offer consistent job opportunities and resilience against economic fluctuations:

1. **Healthcare**: The healthcare industry, including hospitals, clinics, and pharmaceutical companies, tends to remain stable due to ongoing demand for medical services and products regardless of economic conditions.
2. **Education**: Both K-12 education and higher education institutions generally maintain stability as there is a continuous need for educators, administrators, and support staff to serve students.
3. **Government and Public Sector**: Jobs in government agencies at local, state, and federal levels provide stability, often supported by budgets that are less affected by economic cycles.
4. **Utilities**: Utilities such as water, electricity, and natural gas are essential services, ensuring a steady demand for skilled workers in operations, maintenance, and management.
5. **Information Technology (IT)**: The IT industry, including software development, cybersecurity, and tech support, remains robust due to ongoing technological advancements and digital transformation across various sectors.
6. **Financial Services**: Despite fluctuations in financial markets, roles in banking, insurance, and financial planning remain stable due to the essential nature of these services in managing money and mitigating risk.
7. **Telecommunications**: The telecommunications industry, encompassing providers of internet, phone, and wireless services, continues to grow as connectivity becomes increasingly vital in modern society.
8. **Pharmaceuticals and Biotechnology**: Companies involved in

pharmaceuticals, biotech research, and medical devices benefit from continuous demand for healthcare innovations and treatments.

9. **Legal Services**: Legal professionals, including lawyers, paralegals, and legal assistants, are essential in providing counsel and representation, ensuring stability in this sector.

10. **Environmental Services**: As awareness of environmental issues grows, industries focused on environmental sustainability, renewable energy, and waste management offer stable career opportunities.

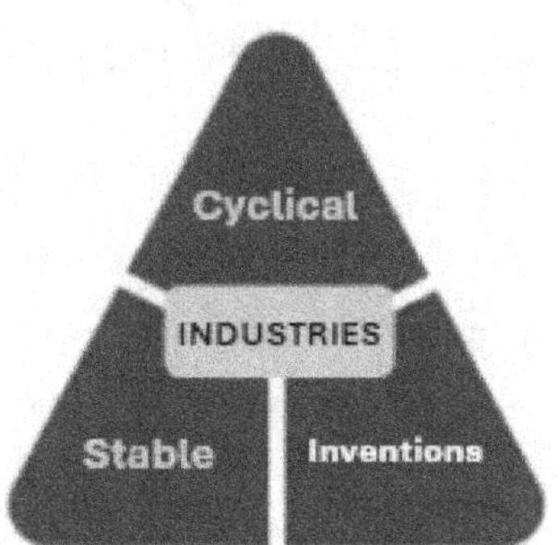

Cyclical
INDUSTRIES
Stable
Inventions

Inventions

Inventing new products and services to start a new trend is like setting sail on a creative adventure where your ideas have the power to shape the future! Whether you're designing a revolutionary gadget, launching a unique service, or introducing a fresh approach to an existing industry, innovation can capture the imagination and interest of consumers. By identifying gaps in the market or anticipating emerging needs and preferences, you can not only meet demand but also lead and define a new trend.

One of the exciting aspects of pioneering new products or services is the potential to make a meaningful impact. Whether it's improving efficiency, enhancing convenience, or promoting sustainability, innovative ideas can address real-world challenges and improve people's lives. This sense of purpose can fuel your passion and drive as you work to bring your vision to fruition.

Moreover, creating something new allows you to showcase your creativity and entrepreneurial spirit. It's about envisioning possibilities, taking calculated risks, and embracing the journey of bringing your ideas to market. Along the way, you'll likely encounter hurdles and setbacks, but each challenge presents an opportunity to learn, iterate, and refine your concept. With perseverance and a willingness to adapt, you can navigate the complexities of launching a new trend-setting product or service, ultimately leaving your mark on the industry and inspiring others to innovate.

Here's a true example of this: A guy named Gary Dahl, an ad executive, heard his friends complain about pet care at home and he came up with the idea of a "Pet Rock." Owners of a Pet Rock don't have to feed, nurture, go to the vet, and so on. He sold over one million of this crazy idea for $4 each and became a millionaire... just on a lark. Who knew this could happen?!

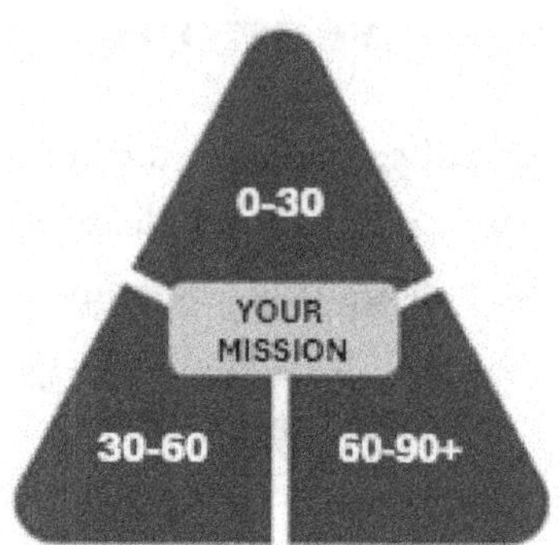
0-30
YOUR
MISSION
30-60
60-90+

YOUR MISSION

The mission of a person's life during their career is like crafting a meaningful story filled with purpose, growth, and impact. It's about discovering and pursuing a path that aligns your talents, passions, and values with the work you do. Your career becomes more than just a series of jobs; it becomes a journey where each role and experience contribute to your personal and professional development.

Central to this mission is the pursuit of fulfillment and contribution. It's about finding work that not only brings you joy and satisfaction but also allows you to make a positive difference in the lives of others. Whether you're in healthcare, education, technology, or any other field, your mission might be to heal, educate, innovate, or serve. When your career is driven by a sense of mission, each day becomes an opportunity to grow, learn, and contribute your unique talents to the world.

Furthermore, the mission of your life during your career involves continuous learning and adaptation. As industries evolve, technologies advance, and societal needs change, embracing lifelong learning ensures that you remain relevant and resilient. It's about seeking new challenges, acquiring new skills, and staying curious and open-minded. By continually expanding your knowledge and expertise, you not only enhance your career prospects but also deepen your impact and relevance in your chosen field. Ultimately, the mission of your life during your career is about crafting a narrative of purpose, growth, and impact—a journey where your professional endeavors contribute to a fulfilling and meaningful life story.

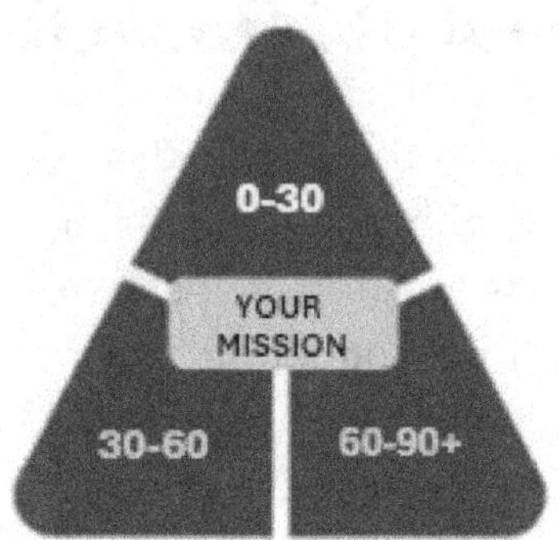
0-30
YOUR
MISSION
30-60
60-90+

0-30

The discovery years, spanning from age 0 to 30, play a pivotal role in shaping our interests, values, and skills, all of which influence our career choices. During this period, we undergo significant developmental milestones—from childhood exploration to adolescent identity formation and early adulthood decision-making. These years are marked by educational experiences, personal interests, hobbies, and interactions with family, friends, and mentors, all of which contribute to our understanding of ourselves and our aspirations for the future.

From a young age, our experiences and environments expose us to different professions and fields. Whether it's through role models, school projects, or extracurricular activities, these early exposures help us develop preferences and inclinations toward certain careers. For instance, a child fascinated by science experiments might grow up to pursue a career in research, while someone passionate about helping others might be drawn to healthcare or social work. These formative years are crucial in sparking our curiosity and laying the foundation for our career interests.

As we transition into adolescence and young adulthood, the discovery years continue to play a significant role in shaping our career paths. This is a time of exploration and experimentation, where we test our skills, pursue higher education, gain work experience through internships or part-time jobs, and refine our career goals. Personal values, such as a desire for creativity, stability, or social impact, often become more pronounced during this period and influence the types of careers we find fulfilling. Ultimately, the discovery years provide a rich tapestry of experiences and influences that guide us toward careers that resonate with our passions, values, and aspirations for the future.

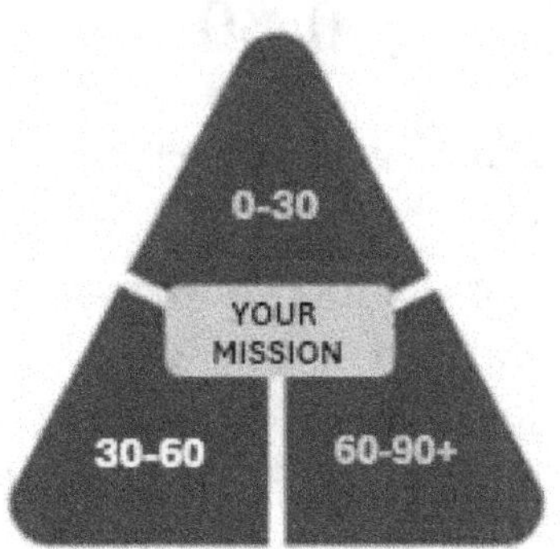
0-30
YOUR
MISSION
30-60
60-90+

30-60

The earning years, spanning from ages 30 to 60, mark a significant phase in a person's career where professional accomplishments and financial stability often take center stage. This period is characterized by leveraging the skills, knowledge, and experience gained earlier in one's career to pursue advancement, higher earnings, and long-term financial goals. It's a time when individuals typically reach their peak earning potential and make strides towards achieving financial security and independence.

During the earning years, many people focus on career progression and professional development. Whether through promotions, expanding responsibilities, or acquiring additional certifications and skills, this period is about maximizing opportunities for growth and advancement. It's common to see individuals taking on leadership roles, mentoring younger colleagues, or exploring entrepreneurial ventures as they capitalize on their expertise and experience.

Moreover, the earning years often coincide with significant life milestones such as buying a home, starting a family, or planning for retirement. This makes financial planning and management crucial during this phase of life. Many individuals prioritize saving for retirement, investing in assets, and ensuring financial stability for themselves and their families. This period may also involve balancing career ambitions with personal priorities, such as maintaining work-life balance and nurturing relationships, to achieve overall well-being and fulfillment.

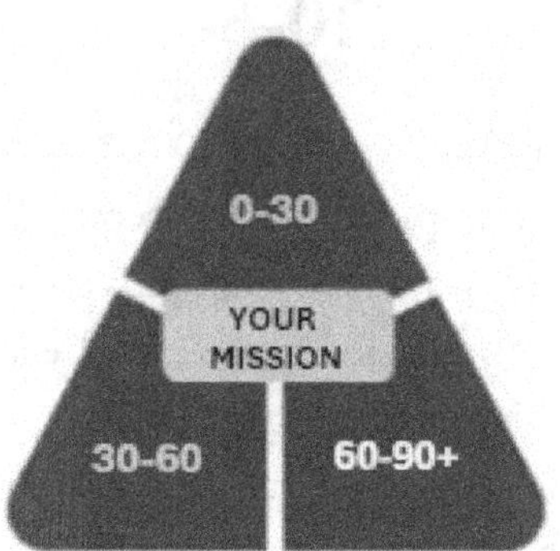
0-30
YOUR
MISSION
30-60
60-90+

60-90+

The philanthropy years, spanning from ages 60 to 90 and beyond, mark a unique phase in a person's career where accumulated wisdom, experience, and resources are often directed towards giving back and making a positive impact on society. This period is characterized by a shift from focusing primarily on personal and professional goals to contributing to causes, organizations, and communities that align with one's values and passions. It's a time when individuals often find fulfillment in leaving a lasting legacy and supporting initiatives that create meaningful change.

During the philanthropy years, many people become actively involved in charitable giving, volunteer work, and advocacy efforts. Whether through donating time, money, or expertise, individuals leverage their skills and resources to address social issues, support education, promote healthcare initiatives, or advance environmental sustainability. This commitment to philanthropy reflects a desire to make a difference and leave the world a better place for future generations.

Moreover, the philanthropy years often involve passing down knowledge and values to younger generations, mentoring aspiring leaders, and fostering a culture of giving within families and communities. Many individuals establish foundations, endowments, or charitable trusts to institutionalize their philanthropic efforts and ensure sustainable support for causes they care about. This period may also include engaging in collaborative partnerships with other philanthropists, nonprofits, and government agencies to amplify impact and tackle complex societal challenges.

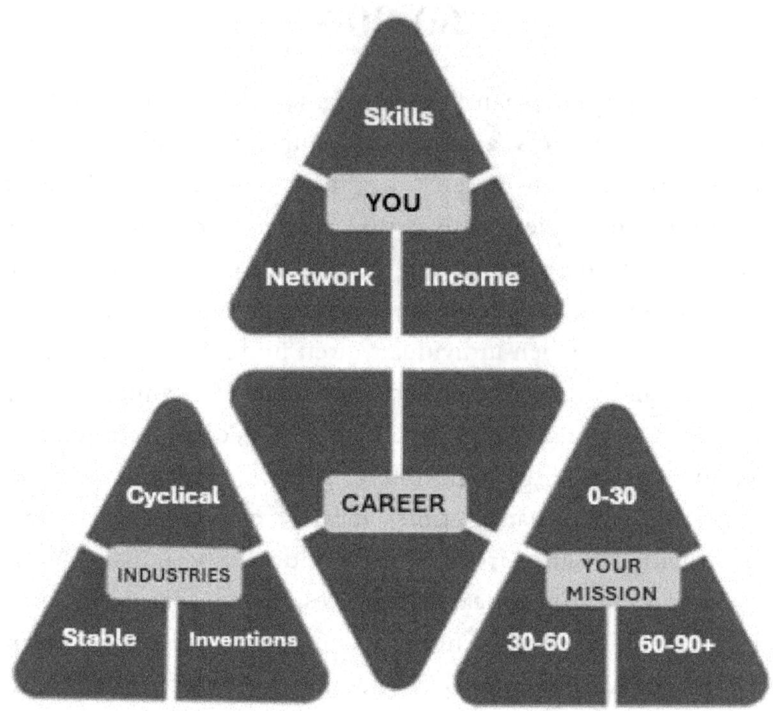
Skills
YOU
Network
Income
Cyclical
INDUSTRIES
Stable
Inventions
CAREER
0-30
YOUR
MISSION
30-60
60-90+

SUMMARY

Remaining flexible throughout your career is like having a superpower that allows you to navigate changes, seize opportunities, and adapt to evolving circumstances with ease. In today's dynamic work environment, industries, technologies, and job roles are constantly evolving. Being open to change and willing to embrace new challenges enables you to stay relevant and resilient in the face of uncertainty. Flexibility allows you to pivot, when necessary, whether it's exploring new career paths, acquiring new skills, or adjusting to changes in the workplace.

Moreover, remaining flexible fosters a mindset of continuous learning and growth. It encourages you to seek out new experiences, take on diverse projects, and expand your capabilities. This not only enhances your professional expertise but also opens doors to new opportunities for advancement and career development. By staying adaptable, you demonstrate to employers and colleagues alike that you are agile, resourceful, and capable of thriving in a rapidly changing world.

Furthermore, flexibility promotes work-life balance and overall well-being. It allows you to adjust your schedule, workload, or job responsibilities to accommodate personal commitments, pursue hobbies, or prioritize self-care. Striking a healthy balance between work and life ensures that you can sustain your energy and enthusiasm over the long term, ultimately contributing to greater job satisfaction and overall happiness. Embracing flexibility in your career journey empowers you to navigate transitions, embrace growth opportunities, and maintain a fulfilling and balanced life both professionally and personally.

Invitation

Making your career planning a priority is like investing in your own success and happiness. Just as you would map out a road trip or plan a vacation, taking the time to strategize and set goals for your career can significantly impact your professional trajectory. By making career planning a priority, you demonstrate a commitment to your future and empower yourself to proactively shape your path.

Firstly, prioritizing career planning involves self-reflection and assessment. It's about understanding your strengths, skills, interests, and values, and aligning them with potential career paths that resonate with you. This introspective process helps you clarify your professional aspirations and identify areas for growth or development. By gaining clarity on your goals and priorities, you can make informed decisions about the steps needed to achieve them.

Secondly, effective career planning includes setting clear and achievable objectives. This involves creating short-term and long-term goals that outline the milestones you want to accomplish in your career journey. Whether it's acquiring specific skills, gaining experience in a new industry, or advancing to a leadership position, setting goals provides direction and motivation. It allows you to track your progress, celebrate achievements, and adjust your strategies as needed to stay on course.

Lastly, making career planning a priority involves taking action and implementing your plan. This may include networking, seeking mentorship, pursuing further education or certifications, and actively applying for opportunities that align with your career goals. By consistently investing time and effort into your professional growth and development, you position yourself for success and create opportunities for advancement and fulfillment in your chosen field. Ultimately, making career planning a priority is an investment in yourself and your future, ensuring that you can navigate challenges, seize opportunities, and build a rewarding and fulfilling career path.

When you're with someone who is sharing their struggles with you...just smile at him/her and give them one of these. He/she will ask "What is that?" Then simply reply "Life Works in Threes."

Other titles coming out:

- Weight Struggles?
- Abundance Struggles?
- Parenting Struggles?
- Life Struggles?
- Purpose Struggles?
- Happiness Struggles?
- Sales Struggles?
- Speaker Struggles?
- Time Struggles?
- Network Struggles?
- Marriage Struggles?
- Divorce Struggles?
- Money Struggles?
- Romance Struggles?
- Dating Struggles?
- Caretaker Struggles?
- Forgiveness Struggles?
- Grieving Struggles?
- Success Struggles?
- Golf Struggles?
- Workplace Struggles?
- Stress Struggles?
- Shame/Guilt Struggles?
- Addiction Struggles?

Remember,
When you get right down to it,

Life is about making choices.

Every day, all day long, that's what we do.

- *We choose to get out of bed or not.*
- *We choose to clean up or not.*
- *We choose what to eat all day.*
- *We choose to exercise or not.*
- *We choose to go to work or not.*
- *We choose to do a good job or not.*
- *We choose to come home or not.*
- *We choose to watch TV or do something constructive.*
- *We choose to bed at a decent hour or not.*

And the next day...we start all over again.

What is the meaning of this? Get good at choosing.

Before you can get good at choosing though...you need to understand how life works in threes.

Quotes about Career

"The best way to predict the future is to create it." - Abraham Lincoln

"Your career is what you're paid for. Your calling is what you're made for." - Unknown

"Don't be afraid to give up the good to go for the great." - John D. Rockefeller

"Choose a job you love, and you will never have to work a day in your life." - Confucius

"Your work is going to fill a large part of your life, and the only way to be truly satisfied is to do what you believe is great work. And the only way to do great work is to love what you do." - Steve Jobs

Preferences for jobs can vary widely among individuals, but here's a list of occupations that have historically seen higher representation of **women**:

1. **Registered Nurse**: Nursing is a field where women have traditionally been well-represented due to caregiving roles and opportunities for advancement.
2. **Elementary School Teacher**: Teaching at the elementary level attracts many women due to a passion for education and nurturing young children.
3. **Social Worker**: Social work involves helping individuals and families overcome challenges, which often attracts women interested in social justice and community support.
4. **Human Resources Specialist**: HR roles involve managing people and policies within organizations, which can appeal to women interested in organizational behavior and workplace dynamics.
5. **Graphic Designer**: Design fields, including graphic design, often see higher participation from women due to creative opportunities and flexible work arrangements.
6. **Psychologist/Counselor**: Psychology and counseling attract women interested in mental health and helping professions.
7. **Accountant/Auditor**: Accounting and auditing offer stable career paths and opportunities for advancement that appeal to many women.
8. **Writer/Editor**: Writing and editing roles can be flexible and creative, making them attractive to women with strong communication skills.

9. **Marketing Manager**: Marketing involves strategic thinking and creativity, areas where many women excel.
10. **Event Planner**: Event planning combines organizational skills with creativity, appealing to women interested in managing details and creating memorable experiences.

These roles are not exclusive to women, and there is increasing diversity across all professions. Preferences can vary based on individual interests, education, and career goals.

Preferences for jobs can vary widely among individuals, but here's a list of occupations that have historically seen higher representation of **men**:

1. **Software Developer / Engineer**: IT and software development roles often attract men due to opportunities for innovation, problem-solving, and high earning potential.
2. **Mechanical Engineer**: Engineering fields, including mechanical engineering, tend to have a higher representation of men due to interest in technical challenges and design.
3. **Electrician**: Skilled trades such as electrician work attract men interested in hands-on, practical work and technical expertise.
4. **Police Officer / Detective**: Law enforcement careers often appeal to men due to the physical and mental challenges, as well as opportunities to serve and protect communities.
5. **Construction Worker**: Construction roles involve physical labor and skill-based work, which traditionally attract more men.
6. **Pilot**: Aviation careers, including commercial pilots and flight engineers, often see higher representation from men due to interest in flying and technical aspects of aviation.
7. **Sales Manager**: Sales management roles can appeal to men due to the competitive nature of sales and opportunities for financial success through commission-based earnings.
8. **Financial Analyst**: Finance and investment roles attract men interested in numbers, analysis, and

financial markets.

9. **Truck Driver**: Transportation and logistics jobs like truck driving typically have more male representation due to the nature of long-haul driving and logistics management.

10. **Mechanic**: Automotive and machinery repair roles attract men interested in hands-on mechanical work and troubleshooting.

It's important to note that these trends are changing, and there is increasing diversity across all professions as societal norms evolve and more individuals pursue careers based on their interests and skills rather than traditional gender roles.

Here's a comprehensive list of things to do when preparing for a job search:

Self-Assessment:

Identify your skills, strengths, weaknesses, and interests.

Determine your career goals and preferences.

Clarify what type of job you are seeking.

Research:

Explore different industries and sectors of interest.

Research companies you would like to work for.

Gather information on job market trends and salary expectations.

Update Your Resume:

Tailor your resume for each job application.

Highlight relevant skills and experience.

Use clear and concise language, avoiding jargon.

Prepare Your Cover Letter:

Write a compelling cover letter that complements your resume.

Customize each cover letter for the specific job and company.

Develop Your Online Presence:

Update your LinkedIn profile with current information and a professional photo.

Clean up any unprofessional social media profiles.

Network:

Reach out to contacts in your industry or field.

Attend networking events, both in person and online.

Join professional associations or groups related to your career interests.

Prepare for Interviews:

Practice common interview questions and answers.

Research the company and its culture.

Prepare questions to ask the interviewer.

Skills Development:

Consider any skills gaps and take steps to address them (courses, certifications, etc.).

Stay updated on industry trends and developments.

Job Search Strategies:

Use job search engines and career websites to find openings.

Set up job alerts for relevant positions.

Consider using recruitment agencies or job fairs.

Organize and Track Applications:

Keep track of jobs you have applied to and their deadlines.

Follow up on applications if necessary.

Keep a record of interviews and feedback received.

Prepare References:

Identify potential references (previous employers, professors, etc.).

Contact them to ask permission to use them as references.

Provide references' contact information when requested.

Financial Preparation:

Consider your financial situation and plan accordingly.

Save for potential periods of unemployment or relocation costs.

Stay Positive and Persistent:

Job searching can be challenging, so maintain a positive attitude.

Be persistent and resilient in your efforts.

By systematically working through these steps, you can effectively prepare for a successful job search and increase your chances of landing the right job for you.

When someone is struggling with a particular area or two, chances are they are "out of balance" with how life works. How does life work? Life works in threes.

If you're interested in personal topics like life, health, money or business topics like sales, time management and public speaking...TRYUNE WORKS! can shed some light on creating success in those areas.

The definition of TRIUNE is a group of three things; united. Being three in one, such as - humans are *mental, physical* and *spiritual beings.* The word TRYUNE is a play of the word TRIUNE, encouraging all to try this concept and help eliminate struggling unnecessarily.

LifeWorksInThrees.com